MEET
THE **KEY**
WORKERS

DELIVERY
WORKERS

BY
SHALINI VALLEPUR

KidHaven
PUBLISHING

Published in 2024 by
KidHaven Publishing, an Imprint of Greenhaven Publishing, LLC
2544 Clinton St., Buffalo, NY 14224

© 2022 Booklife Publishing
This edition is published by arrangement with Booklife Publishing

Written by: Shalini Vallepur
Edited by: John Wood
Designed by: Jasmine Pointer

Cataloging-in-Publication Data

Names: Vallepur, Shalini.
Title: Delivery workers / Shalini Vallepur.
Description: New York : KidHaven Publishing, 2024. |
    Series: Meet the key workers | Includes glossary and
    index.
Identifiers: ISBN 9781534544390 (pbk) |
    ISBN 9781534544406 (library bound) |
    ISBN 9781534544413 (ebook)
Subjects: LCSH: Delivery of goods-- Juvenile literature
    | Mail carriers-- Juvenile literature| Postal service--
    Juvenile literature
Classification: LCC HE6078 V35 2024 |
    DDC 388/.044 --dc23

Manufactured in the United States of America

CPSIA compliance information: Batch #CSKH24: For further information contact Greenhaven Publishing LLC at 1-844-317-7404.

Please visit our website, www.greenhavenpublishing.com. For a free color catalog of all our high-quality books, call toll free 1-844-317-7404 or fax 1-844-317-7405.

Find us on

Image Credits

All images are courtesy of Shutterstock.com, unless otherwise specified. With thanks to Getty Images, Thinkstock Photo and iStockphoto.

Cover – antoniodiaz, Gorodenkoff, SpeedKingz, Juliasart, alazur. 4–5 – LP2 Studio, Monkey Business Images. 6–7 – M_Agency, Gorodenkoff, 8–9 – Stacey Newman, alazur, rlat, Kauka Jarvi, Anatolir. 10–11 – Halfpoint, Gorodenkoff, Zeynur Babayev. 12–13 – May_Chanikran, B.Zhou, H.Elvin. 14–15 – Phoderstock, Bjoern Wylezich, alazur, ideyweb. 16–17 – pcruciatti, Drazen Zigic, YummyBuum. 18–19 – natashanast, Jaromir Chalabala, Avigator Fortuner, Photomarine, Tartila, freshcare. 20–21 – Atstock Productions, Daisy Daisy, LoopAll, Kunturtle, TaMih, Oxy_gen, jehsomwang. 22–23 – 5D Media, Sensvector, iceink, NTL studio, v74.

CONTENTS

Words that look like **this** can be found in the glossary on page 24.

HERE TO HELP

There are lots of jobs in the world and each one is different. Some jobs are always needed. The people who do these jobs are called key workers.

Key can sometimes mean needed and important.

Teachers
are always
needed
to teach
us.

Without key workers, we would not have the things we need to live safely, such as food and important **services**.

PEOPLE IN
DELIVERY

Have you ever sent a letter or **received** a package? People who work in delivery jobs are key workers. We need them to bring letters, packages, and important **goods** like food.

Lots of people work in delivery to make sure everything is received safely and on time. Let's learn about the different people and jobs in delivery!

AT THE
POST OFFICE

When a letter is put into a mailbox, a postal worker goes to collect it. The postal worker may collect mail from many mailboxes in one day.

POST OFFICE

U.S.MAIL

UNITED STATES
POSTAL SERVICE

1951

Large letters and packages must be sent at a post office.
Some postal workers sort through the letters and packages,
while others take them away to be delivered.

AT THE
MAIL CENTER

Mail arrives at a big mail center. Machines sort the mail and packages into groups depending on where they need to go. Workers make sure nothing goes wrong.

Forklift drivers use forklifts to carry mail and other heavy goods around the mail center. They help to load the mail and goods onto trucks and vans.

WORKING AT A
WAREHOUSE

A warehouse is a large building that has lots of goods inside. Some shops and supermarkets keep all their goods in warehouses. When they need the goods, they ask for them to be delivered.

Warehouse workers work hard each day and night to make sure everybody gets what they need. They check that the goods are going to the right place.

ON THE ROAD

Truck drivers drive the goods closer to where they need to be delivered. Mail and goods may be taken to other mail centers where they are checked and sorted by workers again.

When everything is sorted, the mail and goods are ready to be collected by postal workers and sent out for delivery.

OUT FOR DELIVERY!

Postal delivery workers collect mail from a mail center to deliver it. Each postal delivery worker has their own route. This means they may go to the same area every day to deliver mail.

Some postal delivery workers deliver mail and packages by walking. Others may drive cars, vans, or ride a bike.

Postal delivery workers deliver our mail even when it's raining and snowing.

THE SEA AND THE SKY

Some goods are flown **overseas** on **cargo** planes. Workers pack and load the goods onto the plane, which is flown by a pilot.

Some mail and goods need to be sent overseas on cargo ships. Workers load the goods into shipping containers which are lifted onto cargo ships.

Shipping containers

45   45   45   45   45

LOCAL DELIVERY

Some stores may deliver to people who live nearby. Many supermarkets can deliver fresh food straight to people's houses. Supermarket delivery vehicles are built to keep food cold.

MILK

EXCELLENCE. S

XF

Some restaurants deliver cooked food. Delivery drivers collect the food from the restaurant and take it straight to people's houses.

SIGNED, SEALED, DELIVERED

People all over the world work hard to make sure mail is delivered on time. The next time you send something, think about how many people will help to deliver it.

Now you know all about some of the people who work in delivery!
Can you match each job below with the right person?

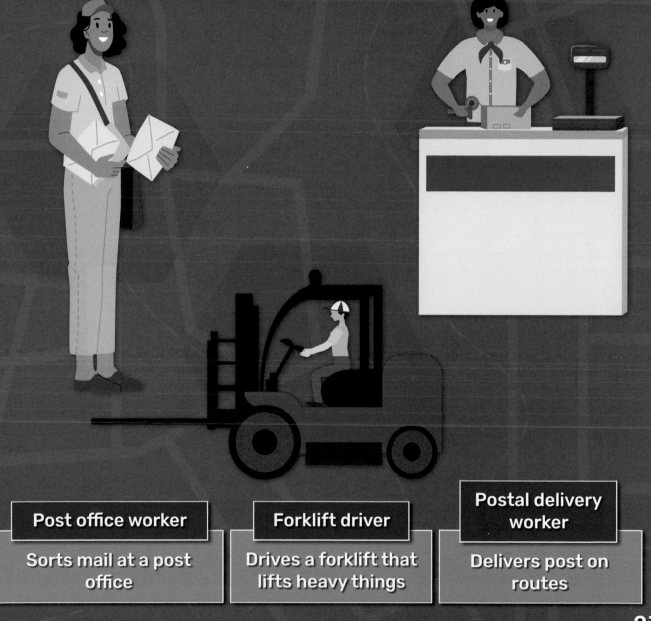

Post office worker
Sorts mail at a post office

Forklift driver
Drives a forklift that lifts heavy things

Postal delivery worker
Delivers post on routes

GLOSSARY

cargo — things that are being transported by a ship or plane

goods — objects that people want and buy, such as food, computers, clothes, and toys

overseas — to a different country, usually one that is across an ocean or sea

received — to have gotten

services — tasks or actions that people pay other people to do, such as caring for older people, fixing things that are broken, or cleaning

INDEX